MANCHESTER: The Warehouse Legacy

An introduction and guide

© English Heritage 2002

Text by Simon Taylor, Malcolm Cooper and P S Barnwell

Photographs by Bob Skingle, Tony Perry and Keith Buck

Aerial photographs by Damian Grady

Photographic printing by Bob Skingle

Drawings by Allan T Adams

Map by Philip Sinton

Survey and research undertaken by Allan T Adams, Keith Buck, Garry Corbett, Ian Goodall, Gillian Green, Bob Skingle, Simon Taylor and Nicola Wray

Edited and brought to press by René Rodgers and Victoria Trainor

Designed by Michael McMann, mm Graphic Design

Printed by Empress Litho Ltd

ISBN: 1 873592 67 1

Product Code: 50668

English Heritage is the Government's statutory advisor on all aspects of the historic environment.

23 Savile Row, London W1S 2ET

www.english-heritage.org.uk

The National Monuments Record is the public archive of English Heritage. All the records and photography created whilst working on this project are available there. For more information contact NMR Enquiry and Research Services, National Monuments Record Centre, Kemble Drive, Swindon SN2 2GZ. Telephone 01793 414600.

MANCHESTER: The Warehouse Legacy

An introduction and guide

Text by Simon Taylor, Malcolm Cooper and P S Barnwell

Photographs by Bob Skingle, Tony Perry and Keith Buck

Aerial photographs by Damian Grady

Photographic printing by Bob Skingle

Drawings by Allan T Adams

Map by Philip Sinton

ENGLISH HERITAGE

Frontispiece The wrought-iron gates to Canada House were made by Princess Art Metal Workers. [AA022686]

CONTENTS

Fig 1 (opposite) Lancaster House (centre), 80 Princess Street, and the adjacent warehouses dominate Whitworth Street and Princess Street. [AA022662]

Manchester and its warehouses

Manchester is known for its cotton mills, the Town Hall and its imposing commercial architecture, but it is textile warehouses that provide the distinctive element in its streetscape and make it unlike any other town in England. These warehouses were only built during the century following 1825 – a relatively short time in the history of Manchester – and were never found throughout the city. However, they are intimately connected with Manchester's past position as the centre for the manufacturing and selling of cotton goods within England and to other parts of the world. Their monumental scale and sometimes exuberant architectural style dominate the areas of the town in which they are clustered (Fig 1). Nowhere else in Britain has there ever been such a concentration of buildings of this kind: the streets of the commercial quarter of Manchester are as distinctive as are those of governmental London.

Medieval Manchester was a relatively insignificant town, but by the 16th century a prosperous class of clothiers and merchants with connections as far afield as London had developed. Two hundred years later, Manchester was the regional centre for textile manufacture and its commercial sector was second only to that of London. Such was the region's importance to this trade that textile salesmen became known as 'Manchester men'. Trade of all kinds was stimulated by improvements in river transport during the 18th century, particularly with the connection of the River Irwell to the Mersey and the port of Liverpool, and by the advent of canals. By 1830, when the town was served by one of the first passenger railways, Manchester had become a great centre of cotton production and was to remain so for the following century. This period was also the beginning of a new phase of rapid economic growth stimulated by the mechanization of cotton weaving. With the growth in trade and industry there was a phenomenal rise in population as more and more people were required to work in both the textile industry and

support trades, and as other kinds of manufacturing were attracted to the burgeoning centre. Along with trade and industry came warehouses, needed to store the food that was brought in to feed the growing population, the imported raw materials (especially cotton) upon which the textile industry depended and the finished products which were to be exported.

Every 19th-century town or city of any size had warehouses, where perishable goods (including foodstuffs) were stored between being brought into the town by the canal and railway and being locally distributed by road. Agricultural and manufactured products also had to be stored, either near the manufactory or close to the transport network, prior to being sent to distant markets. Manchester was no exception in this respect and, as the largest textile-manufacturing town in Britain, had a large number of typical 19th-century warehouses. These catered for all manner of goods, but particularly for clothing and dress accessories made in the town – such as boots and shoes, umbrellas, hats and a whole category of so-called 'Manchester smallwares' (braids, tapes, ribbons, etc). Such buildings, often of modest proportions, were initially concentrated in the Smithfield and Shudehill districts to the north-east of the modern retail centre, on roads such as Dantzic Street, Well Street, Shudehill, Withy Grove, Turner Street, Thomas Street and High Street (Fig 2). Some warehouses were later built further east around Stevenson Square and in the vicinity of Dale Street. Victoria Buildings, built in 1874 to designs by E J Sherwood and R Thomas, accommodated boot and shoemakers' workshops and warehouses (Fig 3). It was arranged on a triangular plan with a central open court and, in 1901, it accommodated a miscellany of enterprises in addition to the shoe factories, including premises for a picture framer and a maker of underclothes, a factory for belts and braces, and a yarn warehouse. Wilson Bothamley's wholesale millinery warehouse had a ground-floor shop below five storeys of storage accommodation and a rear elevation formed by a glazed curtain wall (Fig 4). Newton Buildings, designed by

Fig 2 (opposite, top left) Plain, general-purpose warehouses are common on the minor streets of central Manchester; for example this three-storey warehouse with a full-height recessed loading bay is located in Well Street. [AA006077]

Fig 3 (opposite, right) Victoria Buildings, 6–16 Dantzic Street, was built for multiple occupation, mainly by shoe manufacturers. The many doorways on the main street frontage originally served independent businesses. [AA006080]

Fig 4 (opposite, bottom left) Wilson Bothamley's wholesale millinery warehouse, 58–62 High Street, 1897. Large windows give good light to the upper storage floors. [AA011396]

Charles Clegg and Son and completed in 1907, was a general purpose warehouse which replaced a hatmaker's building (Fig 5).

Towards the end of the 19th century a new series of mail-order enterprises sprang up, bolstered both by the increase in literacy following the 1870 Education Act and by the introduction of cheap parcel post in 1882. Men such as George Oxendale of Northallerton and James David Williams of Derby established companies (Oxendales and J D Williams and Co Ltd respectively) in Manchester, attracted by the volume of its trade and its association with the textile and clothing industries. New warehouses were required to serve these businesses. J D Williams and Co Ltd, for example, constructed Langley Buildings as its headquarters (Fig 6). Designed by R Argile in a baroque style, it is a long, narrow structure of five storeys fronting Dale Street, but with a second display elevation on Hilton Street. Its other façades are utilitarian in character with large windows (Fig 7).

The location in the city of the headquarters of the Co-operative Wholesale Society (CWS), founded in 1863, and of the CWS Bank and the Co-operative Insurance Society subsequently, gave rise to an unusual concentration in Manchester of Co-operative warehouses. These general warehouses came to dominate the northern corner of Shudehill. Though many of the earliest structures have been demolished, a significant number of impressive 20th-century buildings designed by CWS architects survive in the area. For example, three former drapery warehouses – Block E (1902–3) and Federation Building (1913–14) on Balloon Street and Dantzic Building (1937–42) on Dantzic Street – still remain (Fig 8).

While these general warehouses are important both to the history and character of Manchester, the distinctiveness of the city derives from the scale and concentration of carriers' warehouses and the later development of special warehouse forms to serve the textile trade. The carriers' warehouses (*see* pp 7–20), which developed from the mid-18th century, are closely associated with Manchester's growth as the first

Fig 5 (above) Newton Buildings, 50 Newton Street. [AA003190]

Fig 6 (opposite, top) Langley Buildings, 53–5 Dale Street and 34–6 Hilton Street, was a mail-order warehouse. It was designed by R Argile and built in 1908–9 for J D Williams and Co. [Manchester City Council, City Architects, Building Bylaw Plan No. 8424; AA026889]

Fig 7 (opposite, bottom left) Langley Buildings. This view shows the contrast between the elaborate main front and the plain side elevation. [AA003170]

Fig 8 (opposite, bottom right) Federation Building, Balloon Street. This drapery warehouse was one of the impressive group of CWS buildings. [AA006029]

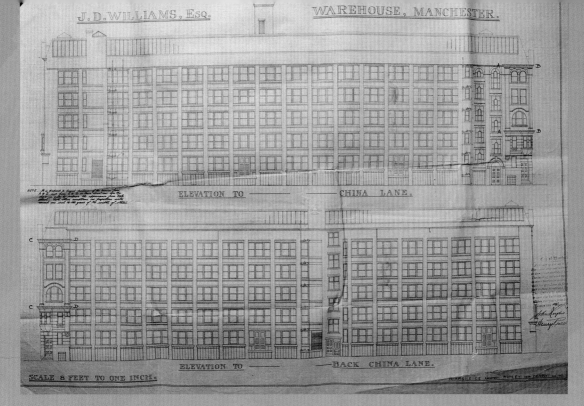

J. D. WILLIAMS, Esq.   WAREHOUSE, MANCHESTER.

ELEVATION TO ——— CHINA LANE.

ELEVATION TO ——— BACK CHINA LANE.

SCALE 8 FEET TO ONE INCH.

industrial city. Their development was intimately connected to improvements in the transport infrastructure, with the development first of canals and then of railways. The size of the carriers' warehouses was what made them distinctive, reflecting the scale of Manchester's economy. Even the surviving, earlier canal warehouses are of considerable proportions – some of the largest buildings erected in the town at the time – while many of the later buildings associated with the railways were conceived on a gigantic scale. The size of these buildings was matched by a sophistication in planning that helped to facilitate the movement of large volumes of goods into, through and out of the warehouses.

The concentration of the cotton industry in Cheshire and Lancashire led to the development of a strong commercial sector in Manchester, reflected in the construction of new kinds of merchants' warehouses from *c* 1825 (*see* pp 20–45). These buildings, conventionally divided into those for the home and foreign trades, were not only used for the storage and trans-shipment of goods, but also accommodated offices, showrooms and areas for quality control and the preparation and packing of cloth for transport. To serve these requirements, new designs evolved. Instead of multiple loading points on the main elevations, a smaller number were less prominently placed, often in secure central yards or wells. In place of small windows, adopted for security reasons, larger ones became more common. The bigger openings were designed to provide as much light as possible in the warerooms where cloth was displayed to customers and checked for flaws in weaving and printing. Instead of utilitarian façades, imposing designs – often of an Italianate style – were adopted as merchants vied with each other to exude confidence and impress their clients and the world at large. Variety in architectural style increased later in the century. It is the buildings of this period, often seven or eight storeys high and with imposing and sometimes exotic façades, which give such a characteristic appearance to the streets of a large part of Manchester's core (Fig 9).

Fig 9 Orient House, 65–7 Granby Row, was a packing warehouse for Barlows Ltd, a makers-up firm and packing company. It was designed by Henry Goldsmith and built in 1912–16. The fine frontage contrasts with the purely utilitarian rear and sides. [AA022619]

The very scale of these buildings, however, means that they pose a significant conservation problem now that the glory days of the cotton industry and trade are over. The warehouses were built at a time when it appeared that cotton would always be central to Manchester's economy, but the severe decline in the trade since the 1920s, particularly in the second half of the 20th century, has meant that surviving warehouses are now rarely used for their original purpose. At the same time, major changes in the supply and transport industries and the requirement for improved storage conditions for many goods left many carriers' warehouses isolated from the main communication arteries, empty and without obvious purpose. Late 20th-century regeneration of the city centre has enabled many warehouses to be converted into flats, offices or hotels (*see* Figs 56 and 58); some are empty or in a state of serious decay, while others have been demolished (*see* Fig 57). Whatever their fate, there has been a degree of loss to the integrity of the historic fabric as conversion usually results in the subdivision of open interiors, the unavoidable removal of some fittings (often of high quality) and alterations to bring the buildings up to modern safety standards. The aim of this booklet is not to suggest that such buildings should be fossilized; that would be unrealistic. Rather, it celebrates what survives, explains the significance of the warehouses and illustrates the unique character they lend to Manchester's streetscape.

Carriers' warehouses

The earliest surviving purpose-built warehouses in Manchester were associated with the new modes of bulk transport that developed during the 18th and 19th centuries. The rapid growth of the town as a centre of cloth marketing and then of textile production depended upon the movement of large quantities of food, fuel and other general goods to support its rising population. Transport and storage facilities were also vital for the import of raw materials (mainly cotton) and the export of finished textiles. The first half of the 18th century saw improvements to the River Irwell, which was made fully navigable all the way to the Mersey and the port of Liverpool by 1736. This was followed in the years after 1759 by the cutting of the Bridgewater Canal, which initiated a series of developments culminating in the opening of the Manchester Ship Canal in 1894, connecting what was by then the City of Manchester to the sea. Over half a century before, in 1830, the link to Liverpool had been revolutionised by the Liverpool and Manchester Railway, ushering in a new age of bulk transport.

The warehouses associated with these transport links were usually built by the contractors who undertook the movement of goods along them. They provided facilities for the storage and, more particularly, the distribution of delicate or perishable goods (such as raw cotton, textiles and foodstuffs) that, unlike coal and timber, could not be kept on open wharves or in yards. Usually, these warehouses were located at the ends of bulk transport routes, where goods were transferred to road wagons for local transport, and they were used for all manner of commodities. Many showed considerable sophistication: some in the way in which materials were moved around within the building and others in the development of warehouse designs that met the particular needs of the three modes of transport.

Fig 10 S and N Buck's The South West Prospect of Manchester, *1728. This drawing depicts cargo vessels on the River Irwell and, on the river bank, a small warehouse called the Rock House. [Reproduced by courtesy of the Director and Librarian, the John Rylands University Library of Manchester]*

River warehouses

Until the 18th-century improvements to the River Irwell, warehouses were not an important feature of Manchester as road carriers generally used inns to store the relatively small quantities of goods they transported. As water transport was developed and the quantity of goods being traded increased, larger storage facilities were required. A drawing of the late 1720s shows cargo vessels moored in the Irwell beside a warehouse, suggesting that the river was an important trading

artery even before 1736 (Fig 10). The warehouse had a three or four-storeyed riverside front rising directly from the water and a projecting crane jib enabled goods to be hoisted into the building directly from the boats through one of a tier of taking-in doors. Goods were then stored, moved through the warehouse and later transferred out of the building on to road vehicles. Evidence of the development of the Irwell as a cargo route following the 1736 link with the Mersey is provided by the establishment of a goods quay slightly upstream of the town a few years later and the connecting of the quay and the town by Deansgate and the newly cut Quay Street.

Most riverside warehouses of the late 18th and the 19th centuries have been demolished but, as late as the 1930s, the Manchester bank of the Irwell from Prince's Bridge to Albert Bridge was still lined with warehouses and goods sheds. Only three now survive. Victoria Warehouse and Albert Warehouse – a pair of five-storey brick buildings of *c* 1840 – have been recently converted into a luxury hotel (Fig 11). The riverside elevation of Victoria Warehouse stands behind a narrow stone quay and has two full tiers of goods doors with projecting pitched covers, while two more face into the yard at the back. The rear wing has a pair of similar tiers on each side and the gable facing Water Street has one large arched entrance. Albert Warehouse is parallel to the quay; its riverside elevation has two round-headed tiers of taking-in doors with a single arched doorway between them, which rises through the first floor. Similar tiers of goods doors face onto the yard at the back. Both warehouses have an internal structure of cast-iron columns supporting wooden beams, joists and floorboards. The other surviving riverside warehouse is the nearby Albert Shed, a large, low, brick and timber structure, which is open to the river and has a canopy sheltering the moorings.

Fig 11 Albert Warehouse (left) *and Victoria Warehouse* (right) *are located on the waterfront of the River Irwell.* [AA026875]

Canal warehouses

As the canal network developed more warehouses were built. Many
were of a new type that permitted boats to be unloaded from within the
building rather than alongside it. The first major warehouse of this kind,
Duke's Warehouse, was built soon after 1765 by the Duke of
Bridgewater at the Castlefield terminus of the Bridgewater Canal and
stood across the head of the canal at Knott Mill Bridge. This warehouse,
as rebuilt after a fire in 1789, is reported to have been 100yds (91.4m)
long. It was demolished in 1919. In 1770–5, the Manchester Grocers'
Company Warehouse (also called Grocers' Warehouse; originally
Hensall, Gilbert and Company's Warehouse) was built beside the
original open coal wharf a little way down the canal. This building was
demolished in 1960 and partially reconstructed in 1987. Both
warehouses had internal docks, made possible by the constancy of the
water level in the canal. Boats entered the buildings through a shipping
hole in the side – a manoeuvre facilitated by the fact that canal boats
had short towing posts rather than tall masts. The Grocers' Warehouse
was five storeys high and had five window bays along the canal front. In
the centre was a single round-headed entrance, rising through two
storeys, where boats entered the warehouse to be unloaded by a water-
powered hoist. Inside, the building was divided in two by a central spine
wall on its long axis, the floor joists extending from there to the exterior
walls without the need for intermediate beams. In 1793 the warehouse
was doubled in length and the upper floors of the two parts were linked.
The extension was not furnished with another internal dock, but was
loaded from the quay. Instead of a spine wall, the new building adopted
a novel design involving a series of internal cross-walls creating a
succession of fireproof compartments through which goods could be
moved across the building.

A little to the west is Merchants' Warehouse, which has a datestone
of 1825 (Fig 12). It is one of only two warehouses at Castlefield that
remains in anything like its original form, despite being damaged by fire

*Fig 12 (opposite) Merchants' Warehouse, Castlefield
Basin, 1825. This warehouse had paired shipping holes
that allowed boats to enter the warehouse directly from
the canal. [AA022677]*

Fig 13 (opposite, top) Middle Warehouse, Middle Basin (Castlefield), 1828–31. The arm of the canal leads to the shipping holes contained within the giant elliptical arch. [AA022679]

Fig 14 (opposite, bottom) Dale Warehouse, Dale Street, 1806. This stone warehouse, built by the Rochdale Canal Company, served the Piccadilly Basin of the Rochdale Canal. The basin has been filled in, but the arches of the shipping holes and wagon entrances can still be seen in the long rear wall. [AA022351]

in 1971 and converted into offices in 1996. Unusually, it lies parallel to the canal rather than across the head of the basin and has both internal docks and canal-side goods doors with external hoists. Like the second phase of Grocers' Warehouse, the interior is divided into transverse compartments. Middle Warehouse, built in 1828–31, is considerably larger (Fig 13). It stands across the head of Middle Basin and now contains luxury apartments and offices. Its canal façade is dominated by a huge elliptical arch containing two shipping holes. To each side of the arch are three bays of tiered goods doors, suggesting that boats were moored alongside, as well as in the internal docks, for loading. Similar doors at the back and in the gable ends would have enabled the movement of goods on the landward sides.

The half-century following the opening of the Rochdale Canal (1798–1804) saw the erection of a number of associated warehouses. Only two have survived – Dale (or Carver's) Warehouse and Jackson's Warehouse – both built by the Rochdale Canal Company near the junction with the Ashton Canal. Dale Warehouse, the first warehouse on the Rochdale Canal in Manchester, stands on Dale Street at the head of what was Piccadilly Basin (Fig 14). It is built of water-shot stone and has four storeys plus an attic and basement. The street front is five bays wide with an elaborate entrance (later obscured by offices) to Dale Street. A datestone in the north gable bears the initials WC, possibly for William Crosley, engineer of the last section of the Canal. On the canal side is a pair of central shipping holes flanked by wagon entrances, while the south end has a tier of goods doors with a covered hoist. A timber dormer above the canal also housed a hoist. In a highly unusual arrangement, the hoists were powered by a subterranean waterwheel installed in 1824. Water was drawn from one of the internal docks and passed into a culvert. It then entered a cast-iron trough leading to the wheel, from which line shafting took power into the 1806 warehouse and into another, nearby warehouse of 1822 (since demolished). Inside Dale Warehouse, cast-iron columns with diagonal struts support

timber beams. The building is now a retail outlet and the waterwheel sits in a chamber beneath a car park.

Jackson's Warehouse, built in 1836, was the last of the canal warehouses constructed in the area (Fig 15). It was named after the carriers on the Rochdale Canal who probably first leased the building during the 1840s. It was built over an arm of the Canal, parallel to Tariff Street (originally Upper Stanley Street). Two shipping holes were flanked by wagon entrances with wide goods doors above; hoists in the roof space allowed goods to be raised to the required floor. There are tiered goods doors in the gable ends and road elevation. The hoists for the latter were hand-powered and had colossal timber capstans and wheels in the roof space (Fig 16); the cable passed to an external pulley mounted under a round-headed hoist cover (cat's head) over each tier of doors. The interior is divided in two by a spine wall (like the first phase of Grocers' Warehouse) rather than being compartmentalised and, within each half, an intermediate row of cast-iron columns supports the floor above. Except on the basement and ground floors, each face of the columns has a slot into which boards could be inserted to divide the space into bins for grain storage (Fig 17).

Railway warehouses

Although the 1830 railway to Liverpool is best known for being one of the world's first passenger railways, it rapidly became a significant transporter of goods. As other railways were constructed during the 19th century, their impact upon the landscape of Manchester came to be as significant as that of the canals. Canal and railway companies competed, especially for the trade to the port of Liverpool. That the relationship between the two modes of transport was immediately clear to contemporaries is apparent from the fact that the Liverpool and Manchester Railway Company attempted to engage the New Quay Company, a carrier on the Mersey and Irwell Navigation, to act as goods carrier and use existing warehouses. More than sixty years later,

Fig 15 (opposite, top) Cutaway drawing of Jackson's Warehouse (1836) on the Rochdale Canal at Tariff Street. This illustration shows how goods were hoisted from boats in the docks, up through the warehouse to the required floor. The goods were then transferred to road vehicles by cat's-head hoists for local dispatch. The hoisting machinery was located on the top floor (see Fig 16). [AA026878]

Fig 16 (opposite, bottom left) Top floor of Jackson's Warehouse. This view shows the capstan, wheel and pulleys that operated one of the cat's-head hoists. [AA022572]

Fig 17 (opposite, bottom right) Second floor of Jackson's Warehouse. This interior view shows the central spine wall (right) and the sack drops in the floor (left). The columns were slotted, allowing boards to be inserted to form bins for grain storage. [AA022575]

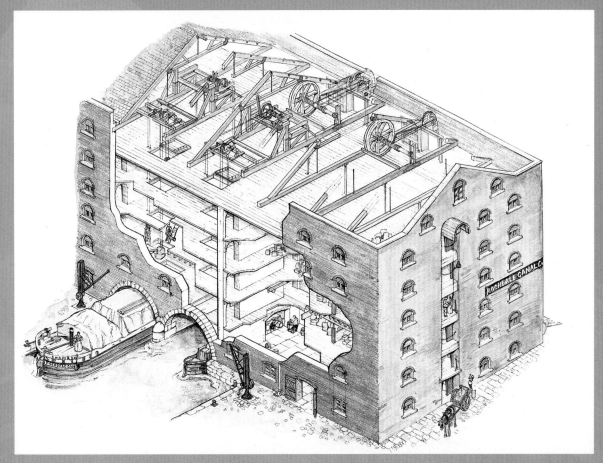

Fig 18 (opposite, top) Liverpool Road Station Warehouse, dated to 1830, now forms part of the Manchester Museum of Science and Industry and much of it is open to the public. This photograph shows the rank of full-height goods doors where goods were transferred to road vehicles. [AA026852]

Fig 19 (opposite, bottom) Liverpool Road Station Warehouse. Interior view of a rail deck. [AA026847]

the Great Northern Railway (GNR) built a vast warehouse complex on a site next to Deansgate, which served as an interchange between the railway, road transport and the Manchester and Salford Canal (and, indirectly, with the Manchester Ship Canal).

Following their failure to engage the New Quay Company as carriers, the directors of the Liverpool and Manchester Railway erected their own warehouses. Their 1830 Liverpool Road Station Warehouse (Fig 18), originally one of five, was the first railway warehouse in the world. Its form was greatly influenced by that of the earlier canal warehouses – its interior being of the same transverse-wall type as the 1793 extension to Grocers' Warehouse – and it was probably designed by Thomas Haigh, adapting a scheme originally intended for Gloucester Docks. The open floor spans were supported on a timber frame, except in the basement where cast-iron columns were used to counter the effects of damp. The long elevations curved with the adjacent railway and there were originally four storeys – a basement, a ground floor accessed from a yard to the north, a first floor accessible from the railway at the south and a second floor. Railway wagons were turned through ninety degrees on turntables and taken into the warehouse through double doors on the first floor (Fig 19). Goods were lifted through the building by gravity hoists and lowered by external hoist to the road below; steam and hydraulic power were introduced later in the century.

By the 1860s railway warehouse designers had broken free of the models supplied by canal warehouses and had turned for inspiration to the fireproof iron and brick multi-storey cotton-spinning mills that were widespread in the Manchester area. In 1865 the London and North Western Railway (LNWR) compelled the Manchester, Sheffield and Lincolnshire Railway (MSLR) to move its goods business from Piccadilly Station (formerly London Road Station). The MSLR, therefore, built a new goods station complex to the west, on land formerly occupied by canal basins and buildings. Only one warehouse

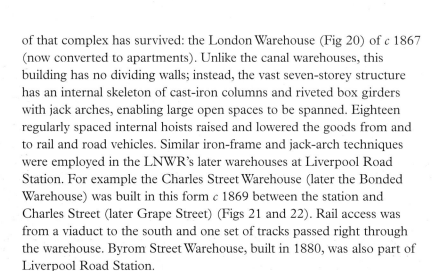

of that complex has survived: the London Warehouse (Fig 20) of *c* 1867 (now converted to apartments). Unlike the canal warehouses, this building has no dividing walls; instead, the vast seven-storey structure has an internal skeleton of cast-iron columns and riveted box girders with jack arches, enabling large open spaces to be spanned. Eighteen regularly spaced internal hoists raised and lowered the goods from and to rail and road vehicles. Similar iron-frame and jack-arch techniques were employed in the LNWR's later warehouses at Liverpool Road Station. For example the Charles Street Warehouse (later the Bonded Warehouse) was built in this form *c* 1869 between the station and Charles Street (later Grape Street) (Figs 21 and 22). Rail access was from a viaduct to the south and one set of tracks passed right through the warehouse. Byrom Street Warehouse, built in 1880, was also part of Liverpool Road Station.

The apogee of the carriers' warehouses was the Great Northern Railway Warehouse, designed by W T Foxlee and built on Deansgate between 1896 and 1899 (Fig 23). It provided an interchange between the railway, the canal system (the Manchester and Salford Canal of 1836–9, which linked with the later Manchester Ship Canal of 1894) and road transport. The railway station was arranged on two levels of the five-storey structure. The main line entered the high-level station where wagons for London were loaded. Wagons for other destinations were loaded below, hauled into the yard by hydraulic capstans and shunted up ramps to the higher level where they were made up into trains. At the north of the warehouse, a dog-leg ramp took road traffic from Watson Street into the high-level station. Below ground level, a new canal basin was excavated, with subways to shafts for hydraulic lifts. The heavy loads demanded a strong framework of steel stanchions, riveted wrought-iron girders and brick arches. This giant complex, which included fine offices, shops and warehouses on Deansgate and Peter Street, was not only the largest, but also the last carriers' warehouse to be erected in Manchester, as the railways were eclipsed by

Fig 20 (opposite, top left) London Warehouse, Ducie Street, was built c *1867 for the MSLR. The great scale and strength of the warehouse is emphasised by its architectural austerity. [AA022596]*

Fig 21 (opposite, top right) Charles Street Warehouse, Liverpool Road Station, c *1869. The decorative brickwork is typical of later railway warehouses. [AA022651]*

Fig 22 (opposite, bottom left) Charles Street Warehouse. The multiple brick arches and riveted wrought-iron beams were capable of taking great weights. [AA022661]

Fig 23 (opposite, bottom right) Great Northern Railway Warehouse: a Bird's Eye View. [From The Railway Engineer, *January 1899, 15; National Railway Museum/Science and Society Picture Library]*

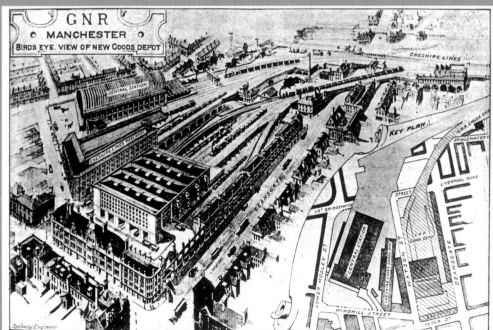

GNR
MANCHESTER
BIRDS EYE VIEW OF NEW GOODS DEPOT

Railway Engineer

road transport. Much of this complex, including the marshalling decks and road ramp, has been demolished, but the principal warehouse (now a retail facility) remains as a reminder of Manchester's great age of industry, canals and railways.

Commercial Warehouses

During the 19th century the immense quantity of cotton cloth and yarn produced in Lancashire and Cheshire was marketed in Manchester, which lay at the heart of a trading system that extended across much of the world. The resilience of demand was such that the trade continued to grow throughout the century. It survived the 1861–4 cotton famine caused by the American Civil War and even expanded through the mid-Victorian recession of the 1870s and 1880s to enjoy a final boom in the early 20th century. Part of the reason for the success of the trade was its ability to find fresh markets in the Far East to compensate for the new industrial competition from Europe and North America that was protected by trade tariffs. However, that same growth of competition, particularly as Asian countries began to process their own textiles, was later to end Manchester's domination of the world market. The decline began in the 1920s and continued through the middle of the 20th century.

The great cotton-spinning mills of Ancoats and other inner city areas of Manchester were mainly constructed in the early 19th century and rapidly came to be regarded by contemporary observers as symbols of a new economic order. The town remained a significant producer of cotton yarn and cloth for the rest of the century, but it was the marketing of textile production from the whole region which came to dominate Manchester's economy. For this reason it is the commercial warehouses, built by the manufacturers, wholesalers, independent

merchants, traders and packing companies during the century after 1840, that are the true symbol of the city's economic character in this period. Many people found employment in warehouses as porters, wagoners and lorry drivers, clerks, makers-up and packers. The buildings themselves became monuments to the importance of the trade, dominating whole neighbourhoods and displaying in their design a remarkable mixture of bold architectural expression and functional pragmatism.

The goods held in the warehouses varied with the nature of the businesses accommodated, but the main items were grey cotton cloth (woven cloth before it was finished), dyed cotton cloth, printed calicos, worsteds, woollens, silk, velvet and all manner of fancy goods. The traders fell into two broad categories: those who dealt with the home trade and those whose interests lay in export; some traders, especially the larger merchant firms and manufacturers, had a share of both markets.

Home-trade merchants and manufacturers often built large, architecturally impressive warehouses that were used as vast wholesale showrooms. Each floor was divided into departments that specialised in certain types of goods and were overseen by a foreman, under whom worked assistants and salesmen. The upper floors were used for the least heavy goods and for those that required the best light for inspection; heavier goods were to be found on the lower floors. Buyers moved between departments to sample and inspect the goods and to place orders. Purchased items were sent by hoist down to a packing room where they were given a final check, invoiced and packed prior to being dispatched. Such was Manchester's dominance of this trade that the goods became known collectively as 'Manchester goods' and the warehouses from which they were bought as 'Manchester warehouses', even when they were in other towns. Warehouses of this kind were distributed throughout the central commercial district of Manchester, though there were particular concentrations on Portland Street and Dale Street.

Fig 24 (opposite) Aerial view of Whitworth Street, Princess Street and the River Medlock from the south-east, showing the dense concentration of packing and shipping warehouses. [NMR 21161/2]

1   Manchester House, 84–6 Princess Street
2   Asia House, 82 Princess Street
3   Lancaster House, 80 Princess Street
4   Cambrian Buildings, 69–71 Whitworth Street
5   India House, 73–5 Whitworth Street
6   Bridgewater House, 58–60 Whitworth Street
7   Dominion House, 48–50 Whitworth Street
8   Central House, 74 Princess Street
9   Lionese House, 54–6 Princess Street
10 104 Bloom Street
11 12 Harter Street
12 Transact House, 48–50 Princess Street and 2 Waterloo Street
13 Rhodesia House, 102 Bloom Street
14 Brazil House, 105–7 Princess Street
15 109 Princess Street
16 61–5 Whitworth Street
17 121 Princess Street
18 Orient House, 65–7 Granby Row

Fig 25 (right) The Royal Exchange closed in 1968, but the trading board, with the last day's prices, still remains. [AA022643]

Export warehouses were also found in all parts of the commercial area, but there were significant clusters on Princess Street and Whitworth Street (Fig 24). Many of the merchants who operated from them were English, but a large number were foreign, particularly German and Greek. The warehouses themselves contained not only storage space, but also offices, rooms for entertaining clients, making-up areas, inspection and packing facilities, and showrooms (though these were less common than in home-trade warehouses). The hub of the export trade was the Cotton Exchange, later called the Royal Exchange. The present Royal Exchange on Exchange Street, built between 1914 and 1921 to designs by Bradshaw, Gass and Hope, is the fourth such building on the site. It closed for the last time in 1968 and now houses the Royal Exchange Theatre (Fig 25). Merchants or their agents met the agents of prospective buyers there to make deals. The merchant then purchased the necessary grey cloth from the manufacturers and sent it out to be printed before taking receipt of the finished goods which were

kept in warerooms in the warehouse. Such rooms were usually lit by large windows and reflective boards were sometimes placed outside to maximise the natural light cast inside. Against the windows were benches on which the cloth was examined by 'cloth lookers' who checked the quality of weave and print and looked for signs of mildew. If there were no problems, the order was made up and sent down to the basement to be packed into bales using hydraulic presses. It was then held until a suitable ship was available and dispatched to port.

Warehouse development

In the late 18th and early 19th centuries merchants stored their goods in their houses. As they prospered and trade expanded, the merchants bought up nearby houses to use as additional warehouse space. Eventually they moved out altogether to live in the suburbs, wholly converting their original houses into warehouses and business premises. This process is illustrated by the development of Mosley Street. It was once the most fashionable residential street in Manchester, lined with 18th-century houses; later virtually all the houses were converted into warehouses before finally being demolished and replaced by purpose-built structures. The new warehouses of the 1820s and 1830s were of utilitarian design: they had all the necessary service facilities, but little or no embellishment. As trade further accelerated, merchants aspired to premises of more impressive appearance to reflect their growing stature and credit worthiness and to impress potential customers. From the 1840s they achieved this by adopting the Italian palazzo style, inspired by the 14th- and 15th-century architecture of Florence, Genoa and Venice. This style was first applied to a warehouse in Manchester in 1839 when Richard Cobden built 14–16 Mosley Street to designs by Edward Walters. It was the dominant style for the next thirty to forty years and, together with subsequent functional refinements, formed a model for warehouses throughout the country.

    The palazzo style changed the face of commercial Manchester,

Fig 26 36 Charlotte Street, dated 1855–6, is a palazzo-style warehouse designed by Edward Walters. This view shows the public entrance on Charlotte Street (right) and the Portland Street entrance to the hovel (left), which extends right through the warehouse. [AA022640]

sweeping away cramped and dingy buildings in favour of elegant and commodious warehouses, thus rivalling or outstripping those of other English towns (Figs 26–29). The windows at different levels of the main façades were often accorded varied architectural treatment, attic storeys were hidden by parapets and balustrades, and decoration and dressings were treated in bold relief. Less visible side and rear elevations, however, tended to be of plainer, more utilitarian design. The interior layout, especially of export warehouses, frequently adhered to a common pattern. Steps led up to a raised ground floor and a main central or corner doorway gave access to a fine staircase rising the full height of the building. Offices and a wareroom or showroom were situated on the ground floor, while the first floor accommodated more offices and sample and pattern rooms, together with waiting rooms for clients. Both the ground and first floors often exhibited a degree of architectural embellishment (for example moulded cornices and panelled doors), thus continuing the display of the showy façades. Above these floors there was less architectural detail and the rooms were used for storing and preparing cloth. Packing took place in the basement, which, because of the raised ground floor, could be lit by pavement-level windows usually protected by iron grilles. In export warehouses the basement contained the hydraulic presses needed to compress the cloth into airless bales for safer shipping, long-term storage and security. The service entrance and workers' staircase were often at the back or side of the building. From the late 1840s such entrances were usually next to an internal loading bay or 'hovel', with a wall crane or 'teagle' and a wagon way to the street. The roadway within the hovel was edged with iron rails and supported by brick jack arches. Internal hovels of this kind were adopted in response to an 1848 by-law. They were introduced partly to relieve congestion on busy roads in a district that had rapidly become dominated by buildings performing the same function and partly for security reasons. Some warehouses continued to have fully external hoist bays and ground-floor goods doors with teagles,

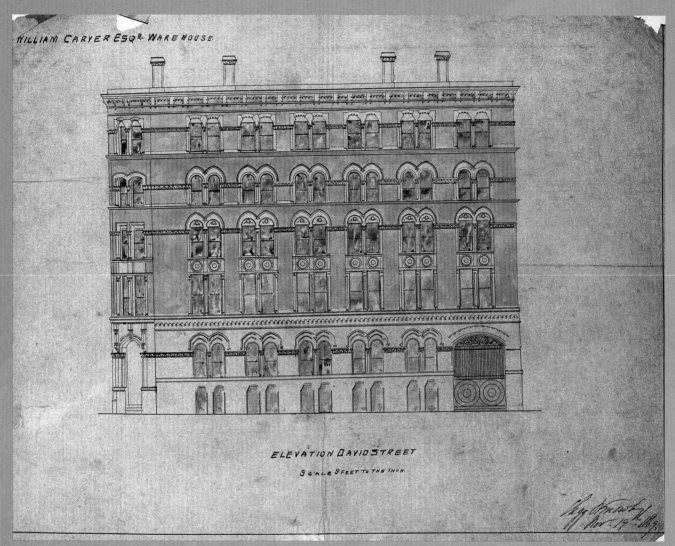

WILLIAM CARVER ESQ^{RE} WAREHOUSE

ELEVATION DAVID STREET

SCALE 8 FEET TO THE INCH.

Fig 27 101 Portland Street was designed by Clegg and Knowles and built for William Carver in 1869–70. This drawing, dated 19 November 1869, shows the David (later Princess) Street elevation with the gated hovel entrance to the bottom right of the building. [Manchester City Council, City Architects, Elevations to New Streets; AA026884]

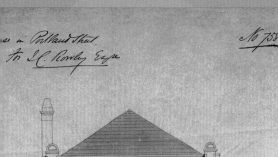

Fig 28 (above) 70–2 Portland Street (first phase) was designed by Pennington and Bridgen and built for J C Rowley in 1869. The building was enlarged in 1873–4 (see Fig 29). [Manchester City Council, City Architects, Building Bylaw Plan No. 396; AA026880]

Fig 29 (right) 70–2 Portland Street as completed by 1874. The right-hand portion of the building, with an elevation to Nicholas Street, was designed for T Hyland by Pennington and Bridgen in 1873. [AA022667]

particularly where loading could be conducted from minor lanes rather than main streets (Figs 30 and 31).

Within the warehouses the movement of cloth between floors was facilitated by hoists. Power for the presses, hoists and cranes was usually hydraulic; the boiler and steam engine needed to work the pumps and maintain the water pressure were under the hovel or in the basement. Artificial light was commonly supplied by gas. The buildings had a framework of cast-iron columns and timber beams that was virtually self-supporting and bore the main load. There were often no joists because the floorboards, which were up to three inches thick and joined together by steel tongues, were so strong that they could be set directly on the beams. This kind of timber flooring, rather than the fireproof brick vaulting employed in textile mills and later railway warehouses, was used partly for reasons of economy, but more particularly because it was thought better suited to the impact and dead loading likely to be experienced in commercial textile warehouses. It was also recognised as being slow burning, although few other precautions were taken against fire; only an enclosed, fireproof stone service staircase and, in later warehouses, a fire hydrant on each floor were usually provided.

In the 1850s some warehouse designers, such as Travis and Mangnall, who designed Watt's Warehouse (Fig 32), began to move away from the pure palazzo style. By the end of the following decade designers drew on an increasing diversity of styles (Figs 33 and 34). There were additional changes in warehouse design from the 1890s and, in the 20th century, these changes were accelerated by the introduction of steel framing, enabling architects to build more storeys and gain maximum return from the plots on which they built (Fig 35). The need for larger warehouses became more pressing following the opening of the Manchester Ship Canal in 1894 and the subsequent establishment of the Port of Manchester. By that time, Manchester Corporation Water Works hydraulic power supply system could provide the power for the machinery necessary to service the buildings.

Fig 30 (opposite, top) Teagles and goods doors at the rear of 70–2 Portland Street (compare with the front elevation in Fig 29). [AA026864]

Fig 31 (opposite, bottom) A deeply recessed, full-height loading bay with a teagle at the rear of 49 Newton Street. [AA022602]

Fig 32 (below) S and J Watt's warehouse, Portland Street, was built in 1851–6. [AA012708]

Fig 33 74 Princess Street was designed in the Scottish
Baronial style by Corson and Aitken in 1880.
[FF000188]

Fig 34 Chepstow House, 16–20 Chepstow Street. This packing warehouse was designed in an eclectic style by Speakman, Son and Hickson and was built in 1874 for Sam Mendel. Mendel did not prosper following the building of his new warehouse and he died in poverty in 1884. [AA022623]

Fig 35 Cambrian Buildings, designed by J D Harker, was built in 1905–7 for J R Jones Ltd. It was constructed at the heart of the concentration of Lloyd's Packing Warehouses Ltd and later became part of Lancaster House. [Manchester City Council, City Architects, Building Bylaw Plan No. 7385; AA026890]

MANCHESTER SHIPPING OFFICES
—AND—
PACKING COMPANY (LIMITED) (Copy)

Submitted & approved at meeting of the Imp? Com?ee 19th June 1885 Benj McLe... Ch

LLOYD STR

SCALE 8 FEET TO AN INCH

Fig 36 (opposite, top) Lloyd's House, Lloyd Street, 1865–8. This building was built for the Manchester Shipping Offices and Packing Company Ltd to designs by Speakman and Charlesworth. This drawing shows part of the Lloyd Street façade and is dated 19 June 1865. [Manchester City Council, City Architects, Elevations to New Streets; AA026897]

Fig 37 (opposite, bottom) Lloyd's House: the service façade to Jackson's Row [AA022613]

With these developments the functional and architectural design of warehouses in Manchester reached its zenith.

Although many firms of export merchants owned and occupied their own warehouses, numerous smaller concerns operated from rented offices and warerooms within larger buildings and subcontracted the making-up and packing of items for dispatch. One of the earliest packing warehouses designed for multiple occupation was the building now known as Lloyd's House (Figs 36 and 37). It is constructed of red brick with stone dressings and Gothic details, and has three storeys plus an attic and basement. A dominant corner turret is located at the top of the main Lloyd Street elevation, which once had numerous public entrances. The original design had another turret on the Jackson's Row elevation, where there are still many goods doors and hovels, each with a teagle.

Lloyd's House was originally built for the Manchester Shipping Offices and Packing Company Ltd. That firm merged with two other concerns in 1896 to form Lloyd's Packing Warehouses Ltd (*see* back cover) and the building was renamed. In the first three decades of the 20th century, when the Manchester cotton trade was enjoying its last boom, the firm built some of the largest and most ambitious warehouses in Manchester. It owned and administered warehouses, offering individual merchants warerooms and office space. It also supplied labour, machinery and space for loading, unloading, storing and packing within the same building and ensured the security and privacy of each of the tenants. The designer of most of these buildings was Harry S Fairhurst, a Blackburn architect who moved his practice to Manchester in 1905 when he received his first commission with Lloyd's Packing Warehouses Ltd. Buildings designed by Fairhurst include India House, Bridgewater House and Lancaster House (Figs 38–40). He was also responsible for York House, Major Street (built in 1911, since demolished), which had an unusual stepped, glazed rear elevation.

The Lloyd's formula proved so successful that by 1923 the

Fig 38 (opposite) India House was built in 1905–9 to designs by Harry S Fairhurst for Lloyd's Packing Warehouses Ltd. Baling holes were situated at the rear of the building. [AA022621]

Fig 39 (above) Bridgewater House was built for Lloyd's Packing Warehouses Ltd in 1912–14. The company monogram is located high on the side elevation. [FF000191]

Fig 40 (right) Lancaster House was built for Lloyd's Packing Warehouses Ltd in 1907–10. The corner entrance was for a small branch of the Union Bank of Manchester and their name still appears in the panel above the door. [AA022605]

company owned fifteen warehouses and the value of the foreign cotton trade it handled represented a third of that trade in Lancashire and was of greater value than the entire export trade of Spain. The concentration of trade in the Whitworth Street area was such that some warehouses even incorporated a bank; Lancaster House once contained a branch of the Union Bank of Manchester (*see* Fig 40).

The way in which a multiple-occupancy warehouse functioned is best illustrated by the example of Asia House, built as a speculation by the Refuge Assurance Company (Fig 41). Asia House was occupied by the Oxford Packing Company and, by 1910, was home to thirty-six shipping merchants. The warehouse is trapezoidal in plan and consists of two distinct blocks, each seven storeys high over a basement and sub-basement and linked together at and below ground level (Fig 42). While the main façade is an exuberant Baroque display in sandstone, brick and marble, the less visible side elevations are of glazed white brick, chosen to amplify the available light, and the rear elevation is of common brick. The main entrance on Princess Street is in the centre of the front façade, while the service entrances are in the side streets. The loading bays are between the blocks and can also be reached from the side streets. These bays have wells at the rear, which enabled goods to be transferred directly to and from the basement (Fig 43). Gated private streets run down each side of the building, allowing access to be tightly controlled and security to be maintained in the private areas. The interior also contrasts architectural richness, seen in the public areas and offices intended for the shipping merchants, with the starkly utilitarian warerooms in which the cloth was checked and stored (Fig 44).

At the junction of Chepstow Street and Oxford Street lay the warehouse estate of H S Booth and Others Ltd, another significant packing firm. The only near-complete survival is Canada House, in which each floor, from the ground floor upwards, was divided by a screened corridor (Fig 45; *see also* frontispiece). On each floor a large open wareroom was at the rear of the building and was served by a pair

Fig 41 (opposite, left) Asia House (right) and Manchester House (left). This pair of packing warehouses, designed by I R E Birkitt, was built in 1906–9 by the Refuge Assurance Company. [AA022304]

Fig 42 (opposite, right) Ground-floor plan of Asia House.

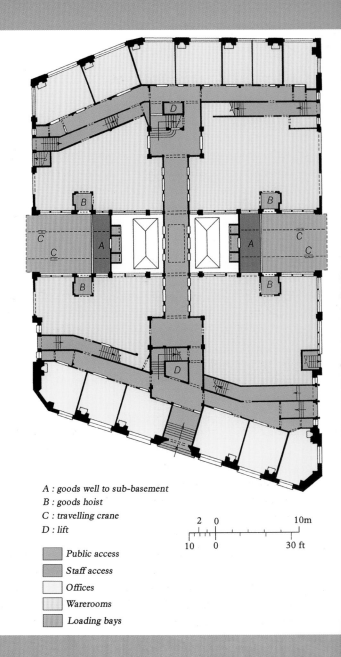

A : goods well to sub-basement
B : goods hoist
C : travelling crane
D : lift

| | 2 | 0 | | 10m |
| 10 | | 0 | | 30 ft |

Public access

Staff access

Offices

Warerooms

Loading bays

ASIA HOUSE · 82 PRINCESS STREET
MANCHESTER   A.T ADAMS JULY 01
SCALE 1:100

Fig 43 (opposite) Cutaway drawing of Asia House. This view shows the north-side loading bay where grey cloth is delivered to the warehouse, via a chute, by a horse-drawn wagon (right). Finished baled cloth is hoisted from the sub-basement for loading onto a steam lorry (centre). A 'cloth looker' inspects cloth on a bench in a first-floor wareroom (left). [AA026879]

Fig 44 (right) Asia House: a view of the fourth-floor wareroom with inspection benches set against the windows. [AA022294]

Fig 45 (below) Canada House, 3 Chepstow Street, 1905–9. This packing warehouse was designed by W and G Higginbottom for H S Booth and Others Ltd. [AA022681]

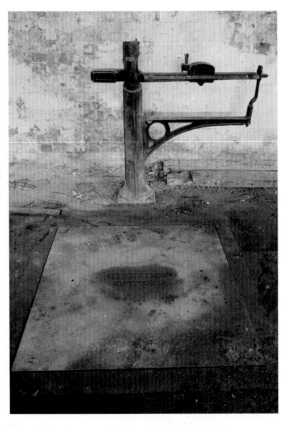

Fig 46 (left) Canada House: a weighing scale in the basement packing room. [AA022700]

Fig 47 (opposite, left) Canada House: hydraulic presses in the basement packing room. Each press was operated by a team of two packers and an apprentice. The hessian strips attached to the press columns held the packers' tools; a partially elevated press table can be seen on the left. [AA022692]

Fig 48 (opposite, right) Canada House: hydraulic press control levers and hydraulic pressure gauge. The water for hydraulic machinery was normally supplied by the Manchester Corporation Water Works at 1100 psi, but water pressure could be boosted by a hydraulic intensifier in the warehouse at times of low power. [AA022697]

of full-height hydraulic goods hoists, while a range of offices was located across the front. Weighing, packing and baling of cloth was conducted in the basement, where a rank of hydraulic presses still remains, prior to the cloth being hydraulically hoisted to a loading bay from which it was loaded onto vehicles by externally mounted teagles (Figs 46–48).

Most of the commercial textile warehouses examined so far were built or occupied by independent merchant concerns, but a significant number of manufacturers also built warehouses and offices in

Fig 49 (opposite, left) The earliest phase of the Tootal, Broadhurst and Lee Building, 56 Oxford Street, was built in 1896 by J Gibbons Sankey. [AA022644]

Fig 50 (opposite, right) Tootal, Broadhurst and Lee Building. This photograph of the first floor of the warehouse was taken in 1900. [BL 15891; Reproduced by permission of English Heritage.NMR]

Fig 51 (opposite, bottom) Tootal, Broadhurst and Lee Building. This photograph of the packing room was taken in 1900. In the foreground are packing cases, destined for the army in South Africa, and three hydraulic presses can be seen in the background. [BL 15888; Reproduced by permission of English Heritage.NMR]

Fig 52 (right) Dale House, 35 Dale Street. This building was designed by J W Beaumont. [AA003175]

Manchester in an attempt to retain control of their markets. For example Tootal, Broadhurst and Lee, a Bolton firm of cotton spinners and manufacturers, began constructing warehouses and offices on and running back from Oxford Street in 1896 (Figs 49–51). Horrockses and Crewdson of Preston and Bolton employed Charles Heathcote to draw up plans for a warehouse at 107 Piccadilly in 1899 and another at the junction of Dale Street and Lena Street in 1901. Richard Haworth, cotton spinner and manufacturer, built Dale House in 1900–3 (Fig 52).

This last warehouse is of six storeys and is faced with grey granite and pink terracotta. A full-width internal roadway for loading and unloading goods from lorries and wagons lies at the back. Thirty years later, in 1930, the old established firm of Rylands and Sons Ltd built a new wholesale warehouse on the corner of Market Street and High Street (Fig 53). The seven-storey Rylands Building (now a department store) has a Portland stone-faced steel frame with towers at the front corners.

Rylands Building was one of the last great textile warehouses to be built in Manchester. By 1930 the cotton trade had begun the precipitous decline that led to the closure of all the great merchant houses. One of the few surviving businesses is Bachers of Manchester, originally a lace merchants at 42a High Street. It is now a wholesale and retail drapers based in 58–62 High Street, a building originally designed as a warehouse and shop for the wholesale millinery firm of Wilson Bothamley and Son in 1897 (*see* Fig 4). The firm of Albert Jones (Textiles) Ltd also remains and is found at 51–3 Richmond Street (Figs 54 and 55).

Although they are no longer used for their original purposes, the surviving warehouses speak of Manchester's first great commercial age and bear witness to the industry and ingenuity of the people who made Manchester the centre of the global cotton trade. Their dominating presence is part of what made and continues to make Manchester unique. Sensitively refurbished and converted for the purposes of a very different age, they can still make an important contribution to the character and identity of the city as it enters a new century.

Fig 53 (above) Rylands Building, 1930. This building was designed by Harry S Fairhurst and his son, P Garland Fairhurst. [FF000155]

Fig 54 (opposite, top) 51–3 Richmond Street. This building was previously a shirt factory, but it became the home of Albert Jones Textiles (est 1905) in 1946. [AA022628]

Fig 55 (opposite, bottom) 51–3 Richmond Street. Interior. [AA022638]

The changing face of Manchester's warehouses

In common with many cities, Manchester has seen significant phases of expansion and decline, each having its own particular influence on the city's built environment. In terms of its later history, it would be difficult to overstate the impact of the cotton industry which, combined with the development of the canal and the railway network, led to Manchester becoming the world's first industrial city. In 1842 its reputation brought Engels to Manchester for two years, during which time he studied industrial capitalism and wrote *The Condition of the Working Classes in England*. The creation of the Manchester Museum of Science and Industry in 1983 and the inclusion of Manchester and Salford (Ancoats, Castlefield and Worsley) on the 1999 tentative list of UK World Heritage Sites have both drawn attention to the national and international importance of the city's industrial history and its buildings.

The catastrophic decline of the cotton industry in the second quarter of the 20th century resulted in the many buildings associated with the industry being subjected to a range of fates from adaptation through dereliction to total loss. Urban change is a necessary and continuing process; it is certainly not new, as illustrated by the case of Mosley Street (*see* p 24). As the city continues to develop and change, however, the survival of its warehouses remains the subject of continuing debate.

English Heritage's wider work in urban areas across England has shown the importance of characterisation as the basis for developing suitable development proposals, whether for individual buildings or for larger area schemes. By characterisation, we mean assessing what it is that makes a place special. There can be no doubt that Manchester's warehouses are historically significant, but one only has to walk down Princess Street, Whitworth Street or into Castlefield, for example, to

recognise the important contribution the warehouses make to Manchester's cityscape in terms of form, scale and design. They give the city its unique sense of place and local distinctiveness: qualities that are not simply of academic interest, but are also of high value for local communities and visitors.

Recent study of the warehouses in Manchester has enabled us to identify and understand the elements of individual buildings that contribute to their special interest and also to assess whether further statutory protection is appropriate. Although there are Grade I warehouses in Manchester, a significant number are listed at Grade II*, including the spectacular Watt's Warehouse (now the Britannia Hotel; *see* Fig 32) and the export warehouses, India House and Lancaster House (*see* Figs 38 and 40). Many other warehouses are Grade II. A number of unlisted warehouses gain protection through their location within the city's conservation areas; government guidance and local planning policies seek to protect unlisted buildings where they make a positive contribution to the character and appearance of a conservation area.

Statutory protection does not always allow the full preservation of historic buildings. Listing and the listed building consent procedure allow for change, but in a considered, managed way. The continuing challenge for developers and those involved in the planning process is to find new uses which are not only sympathetic to the special interest of a building, but which also generate the means to fund immediate as well as long-term maintenance and repair. There have been regrettable cases where the special interest of warehouses has been damaged; often this has happened through lack of understanding that has allowed the erosion of character through incremental change. This book should provide the understanding to inform future decisions.

In general terms the scale and form of Manchester's warehouses have facilitated successful adaptive reuse. The amount of flexibility in adaptation depends in part on the date of the building and its original function, both of which were important factors in determining its form.

For example the earlier canal warehouses tend to have low floor-to-ceiling heights and smaller window openings. Both can pose a challenge in terms of adaptation for new uses and for the introduction of services and other facilities – the systems for fire prevention, information technology, ventilation, heating and sanitation that are required for office or residential use. The relatively low number of window openings presents further problems, as exemplified by Dale Warehouse (Grade II*), where a careful approach to its adaptation will be needed to minimise the level of internal and external alteration (*see* Fig 14). In the case of Merchants' Warehouse in Castlefield (*see* Fig 12), now in office use, servicing has been achieved by the addition of glass blocks at either end of the building. Light is brought into the interior by the use of glazing in the original loading bays and by introducing glazed floor areas and increased roof lighting to transmit the light down to the interior.

The later cotton warehouses, such as the palazzo-style warehouses on Princess Street (Fig 56) and the later export warehouses on Whitworth Street, have greater floor-to-ceiling heights and larger areas of glazing and have proved attractive for new office, hotel, residential and mixed uses. For example English Heritage's North West regional office is based in Canada House on Chepstow Street, an early 20th-century shipping warehouse with very large windows (*see* Figs 45–48).

There has been a range of approaches to adaptive reuse, including those that retain only a minimum of historic fabric. There are examples of façadism (the retention of only the front elevation of a building with a new structure being created behind) and of the retention of the shell of a building around a new internal structure. Some of these schemes have been justified on the grounds of economic viability or due to the need to meet modern servicing and building regulations requirements. Vulnerable internal features include secondary staircases, removed in order to provide space for new lifts and escape stairs.

A lack of appreciation of the value of original features and their

Fig 56 109 Princess Street, 1863–4. This palazzo-style warehouse was converted into a bar and apartments. [AA022671]

attractiveness to occupiers also led to a tendency to conceal historic fabric behind false ceilings and linings in some early schemes. The only hints that the interiors of some converted warehouses retain historic fabric are provided by dropped ceilings that cut across the tops of window openings or suddenly turn upwards at the edges to meet the heads of windows. Fittings such as hydraulic presses and lifting gear are also vulnerable to removal unless understanding of their significance leads to their incorporation into new schemes as interesting features.

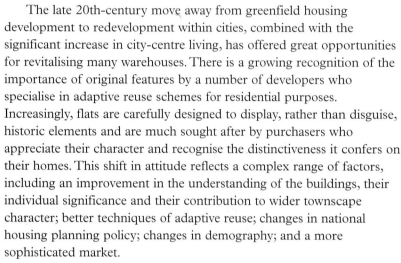

The late 20th-century move away from greenfield housing development to redevelopment within cities, combined with the significant increase in city-centre living, has offered great opportunities for revitalising many warehouses. There is a growing recognition of the importance of original features by a number of developers who specialise in adaptive reuse schemes for residential purposes. Increasingly, flats are carefully designed to display, rather than disguise, historic elements and are much sought after by purchasers who appreciate their character and recognise the distinctiveness it confers on their homes. This shift in attitude reflects a complex range of factors, including an improvement in the understanding of the buildings, their individual significance and their contribution to wider townscape character; better techniques of adaptive reuse; changes in national housing planning policy; changes in demography; and a more sophisticated market.

Despite these changes it would be complacent to conclude that the warehouses of Manchester are no longer under threat. There are still significant challenges. The setting of some historic warehouses has been compromised by adjacent new buildings which overwhelm them in form, material and design. Economic viability and the impact of adaptive reuse still present difficulties. This is especially so where the conservation and adaptation of a specific warehouse not only poses technical difficulties for inexperienced developers, but poor condition also adds to the cost of refurbishment (Fig 57). In a number of cases, such arguments have been used in support of plans which propose inappropriate changes such as the introduction of additional storeys or a penthouse level, the removal of significant internal structures including floors, partitions or supporting columns, or inappropriate external alterations. Such issues are exacerbated where the owner/developer has paid an artificially high price for the building based on a 'hope value', rather than on the careful calculation of the likely costs of conservation (including retention of historic fabric) and conversion.

Fig 57 An unconverted warehouse of the 1850s at 35 Back Piccadilly. [AA022616]

English Heritage recognises the role of the local authority in encouraging and supporting regeneration and reuse, which offer the potential of new jobs, economic activity, new dwellings and an improved quality of life. However, this must be balanced by careful scrutiny of the overall scheme and the financial justifications given for introducing significant levels of change to ensure that where such alterations are accepted, they take account of the special character of the building and are robustly justified.

To assist this process, English Heritage has prepared two detailed guidance notes. *Informed Conservation* (2001) explores best practice for

understanding historic buildings and places as part of their conservation and adaptive reuse, while *Enabling Development and the Conservation of Heritage Assets* (2001) identifies common pitfalls in conservation-led regeneration and provides practical guidance on issues such as viability. However, there seems little doubt that without the continuing vigilance on the part of local authority officers and their planning committees, further schemes that could cause great damage to the remaining buildings will be brought forward and justified on economic grounds.

At the time of writing we have seen a continuing programme of adaptive reuse of warehouses, both for mixed-use development and for residential and hotel schemes (Fig 58). Successful mixed-use schemes may combine ground-floor shops, restaurants, bars or health and fitness clubs, with office or residential space above. The preparation for the 2002 Commonwealth Games in Manchester has led to a number of speculative hotel developments in warehouses, but it has yet to be demonstrated that the market for the number of hotel bedrooms in Manchester provides a sustainable medium or long-term use. Similarly, while there is clearly a continuing demand for city-centre living it is not clear whether this trend (from fewer than 1,000 living in the city centre in 1991 to a projected 10,000 in 2002) is sustainable in the longer term.

The warehouses of Manchester provide a unique resource for those who live and work there and, increasingly, for visitors to the city. They are witness to the city's internationally important industrial and economic development; particularly distinctive are the mid-19th- to early 20th-century buildings which exhibit a characteristic and flamboyant style. Indeed, it is difficult to envisage Manchester without its warehouses and any loss will erode the particular character and identity of the city. The challenge for Manchester, as with all cities, is to continue to take careful and informed decisions about these buildings, recognising and giving weight to their individual importance and the contribution they make to the wider cityscape.

Fig 58 (opposite) Joshua Hoyle's warehouse at 38–50 Piccadilly was built in 1904 by Charles Heathcote. This steel-framed warehouse is now the Malmaison Hotel. [AA022354]

Further reading

Clark, K 2001 *Informed Conservation: Understanding Historic Buildings and Their Landscapes for Conservation*. London: English Heritage

Cooper, A V 1991 'The Manchester Commercial Textile Warehouse, 1780–1914: A Study of its Typology and Practical Development'. Unpublished PhD thesis, Manchester Polytechnic in collaboration with Manchester School of Architecture

English Heritage 2001 *Enabling Development and the Conservation of Heritage Assets*. London: English Heritage

Farnie, D A 1979 *The English Cotton Industry and the World Market 1815–1896*. Oxford: Clarendon Press

Fitzgerald, R S 1980 *Liverpool Road Station, Manchester: An Historical and Archaeological Survey*. Manchester: Manchester University Press in association with the Royal Commission on the Historical Monuments of England

Hartwell, C 2001 *Manchester* (Pevsner Architectural Guides). London: Penguin Books

Kidd, A 1993 *Manchester*. Keele: Keele University Press

McNeil, R and George, A D 1997 *The Heritage Atlas 3: Warehouse Album*. Manchester: The Field Archaeology Centre, University of Manchester

Nevell, M and Walker, J 2001 *Portland Basin and the Archaeology of the Canal Warehouse*. Manchester: Manchester Tameside Metropolitan Borough Council with the University of Manchester Archaeology Unit

Parkinson-Bailey, J J 2000 *Manchester: An architectural history*. Manchester: Manchester University Press

Front cover Lancaster House. [AA022604]

Back cover An example of the monograms used by Lloyd's Packing Warehouses Ltd, Lancaster House. [AA026874]

Inside front cover Middle Warehouse. [AA022679]

The map (opposite) *shows the extant warehouses referred to or illustrated in the text.*